D0503565

Communities Around the World

Shingu

Japan

Elspeth Leacock

PICTURE CREDITS
Cover PhotoDisc/Getty Images; Cover (inset), pages 2 (top), 3, 4, 11 (top and middle), 12–13 (middle), 18, 19 (top and bottom), 20–21, 23, 24 Courtesy/Shingu Sister City Association; pages 1, 2 (bottom) Sharon Hoogstraten; page 5 (bottom), 11 (bottom), 22 (left) Photonica; page 5 (top) Courtesy/Asa Thompson; pages 6 (top), 8–9, 9 (right), 10, 12, 14, 15 (top), 16–17 Koji Kusumoto; page 6 (bottom) The Granger Collection, New York; pages 12 (top), 17 Cameramann International, Ltd.; page 13 (right) AP Wide World Photos; page 15 (middle and bottom) 2002 Cameramann International, Ltd.; page 16 Gary Conner/Photo Edit, Inc.; page 21 (right) Kenneth Hamm/Photo Japan; page 22 (top right) Courtesy/Santa Cruz Sister Cities; page 22 (top background) Magellan Geographix/PictureQuest; page 22 (bottom right) FPG International/Getty Images.

Maps:
Dave Stevenson

Produced through the worldwide resources of the National Geographic Society, John M. Fahey, Jr., President and Chief Executive Officer; Gilbert M. Grosvenor, Chairman of the Board; Nina D. Hoffman, Executive Vice President and President, Books and School Publishing.

PREPARED BY NATIONAL GEOGRAPHIC SCHOOL PUBLISHING
Ericka Markman, Senior Vice President; Steve Mico, Vice President and Editorial Director; Matt Wascavage, Manager of Publishing Services; Marianne Hiland, Editorial Manager; Jim Hiscott, Design Manager; Kristin Hanneman, Illustrations Manager; Sean Philpotts, Production Manager.

Production: Clifton M. Brown III, Manufacturing and Quality Control

PROGRAM DEVELOPMENT
Gare Thompson Associates, Inc.

BOOK DEVELOPMENT
Thomas Nieman, Inc.

CONSULTANTS/REVIEWERS
Dr. Margit E. McGuire, School of Education, Seattle University, Seattle, Washington
Office of the Mayor, Shingu City
Shingu Sister City Association
Santa Cruz City Sister Cities Committee

BOOK DESIGN
Steven Curtis Design, Inc.

Published by the National Geographic Society
1145 17th Street, N.W.
Washington, D.C. 20036–4688

ISBN: 0-7922-8610-3

Fourth Printing September 2005
Printed in Canada

Table of Contents

Seacoast near Shingu

Welcome to Shingu,

a community in Japan. Hi! Or, as we say here, "Konnichi wa!"
(kohn-nee-chee wah). Read that again, out loud! You are
saying "Hello" in Japanese.

こんにちは

"Konnichi wa" in Japanese characters

*My name is
Reiko. I live here
in Shingu, and I
would like you to
come and visit.*

First, I'll show you how we use the **natural
resources** of the sea and land here in Japan—
both old ways and new.

Next, we'll visit the places where I spend most
of my time—school and home.

Last, I'll give you a tour of Shingu. We'll
go downtown to see the shops. We'll visit
some of the interesting places in Shingu
and nearby. I'll tell you about our
beliefs and how we govern ourselves.
You'll meet new people along the
way. Don't forget to greet them by
saying, "Konnichi wa!"

CHAPTER 1

Using Sea and Land

An Island Country

Shingu is in Japan, a country in Asia. To find Japan on a world map, first find Asia. That's easy. Just look for the biggest **continent** on Earth. Then look for the large group of islands off the northeast coast of Asia. That's Japan.

To find Shingu on a map of Japan, first find the largest island. Shingu is on the southeast coast of this island. Can you find it?

Japan is surrounded by water. We have always used the sea as a resource. Our country has many mountains. Mountains are not good for farming, but they are another kind of resource. Many trees grow on our mountains. We use these forests for **logging**. Let's see how we use these resources.

Typhoon!

Shingu has very mild weather. Spring comes early here, and flowers bloom even in winter. But sometimes we do get storms. Do you know what a **typhoon** is? It is a huge storm with waves that can sink boats and winds that can blow down big trees. In your country these storms are called hurricanes. In the western Pacific region, such storms are called typhoons. Sometimes we have a typhoon emergency here in Shingu.

"The Great Wave" by the famous Japanese artist Hokusai

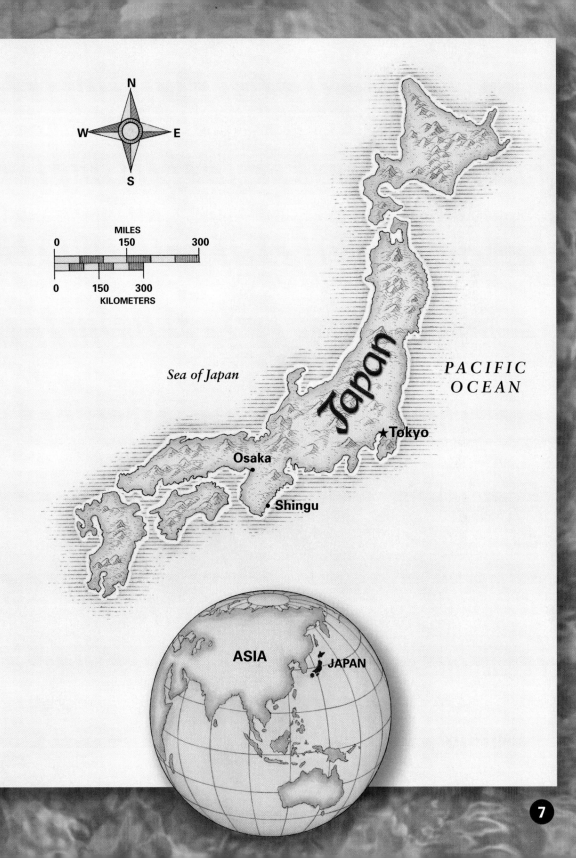

N

W   E

S

MILES
0   150   300

0   150   300
KILOMETERS

Sea of Japan

Japan

PACIFIC
OCEAN

★ Tokyo

Osaka

Shingu

ASIA   JAPAN

Old Ways

In Shingu we live on the seacoast, so fishing was very important to us in the past. It's less important today. But my grandfather still fishes for a living. Sometimes I join him on his boat. Want to come along? We'll have to get up early! He goes out just after three in the morning.

Several boats go to a fishing spot a long way out. There is nothing but the sea and the rising sun. Did you remember a hat? You'll get sunburned without it. What kinds of fish do we catch? You probably know tuna, mackerel, and lobster. Have you ever eaten fish such as bonito, or bream, or cutlassfish, or saury? What about shellfish such as abalone or turban shell? We catch all these.

We return to Shingu in the afternoon. Then my grandfather and the other fishers sell their catch at the local market. Sometimes they catch more than they can sell here. Then they might send fish to the market in our nearest big city, Osaka.

A Shingu fishing boat

The mountains near Shingu have many beautiful forests. Long ago, the area was called "the country of trees." So logging was important to us.

Years ago, after the loggers cut down the trees, they tied them together to form rafts. Then they rode the rafts down the Kumano River. The river carried the log rafts down to Shingu. Then the lumber would be sold at a big sale on the river bank here.

Things are different now. A dam was built upstream, and better forest roads were built. So now logs are shipped by truck. But people still enjoy the excitement of riding the log rafts. Rafting down the river has become a tourist attraction!

Log rafting on the Kumano River

New Ways

Fishing and logging are still done in Shingu. But now we make our living in other new ways too. There are many stores and restaurants in Shingu. People come here from nearby towns to shop and eat.

My father and mother own a **sushi** restaurant. Sushi is bite-size cakes of cold boiled rice seasoned with vinegar. It is rolled up in seaweed or topped with raw fish. My father is the cook. He makes many different kinds of sushi. My mother serves the customers. Sometimes they hire extra help when the restaurant is very busy.

My father gets up early in the morning to go to the market. There he buys the fish and vegetables he uses. For sushi, everything must be very, very fresh! He comes home to have breakfast with us.

He opens the restaurant around ten o'clock. He closes the restaurant after lunch and comes home to rest until four o'clock. Then he returns to the restaurant to serve his dinner customers.

sanma sushi

mehari sushi

There are so many different kinds of sushi!

Sushi

In Shingu, we are famous for two special kinds of sushi—sanma sushi and mehari sushi.

To make sanma sushi, we use fish called saury. A whole saury is placed on rice seasoned with vinegar. Then it's cut into bite-size pieces.

Mehari sushi is a ball of rice wrapped in a leaf with a salty taste. Our loggers used to take mehari sushi to the woods with them for lunch. The name "mehari" means "to open eyes wide." When the loggers opened their mouths wide to eat, their eyes got big too. Try it!

CHAPTER 2

At School and Home

A Day at School

It's 8:30 and time to go inside my school. Please take your shoes off. Leave them in the shoe box at the door. Everyone wears slippers inside.

We have reading, writing, and math. We also have social studies, science, and gym. We have art and music too.

You learned all of your ABCs in the first grade. But your alphabet has only 26 letters. Japanese words are written with **kanji** characters. There are nearly 2,000 kanji characters. Each one stands for a single word or idea. By the time we finish grade school, we must learn over 1,000 kanji characters. Whew! Learning to read and write is a real big job in Japan.

We have recess twice a day. On nice days we go outside and play games such as soccer or dodgeball. On rainy days we stay indoors and talk or read or draw.

We don't only do schoolwork. We work to keep our school nice and clean too. We sweep and dust the classrooms. We also serve food at lunch and then we help to clean the lunchroom up.

Earthquake Drill!

It's an earthquake drill. Quick, get under a desk. These desks are strong and could help to keep you safe if there was a real earthquake. During drills, you might also wear a hood that would protect your head in a real earthquake. Japan is in the **"Ring of Fire,"** an area where there are many **volcanoes** and earthquakes. The Ring of Fire circles the whole Pacific Ocean.

An earthquake drill

My Home

This is the home of my family. Please, come inside. But remember to take your shoes off in the front hall first.

Our home is not big, but it has everything we need. Here is the kitchen where we eat. Tonight we're having soup, tea, and sushi. We're also having pickled plums. The area around Shingu is famous for pickled plums. Some people think they are too sour and salty. But I like them.

Let's go to the living room and watch TV. At night the living room becomes a sleeping room. When we want to sleep, we take a **futon** out of the closet. A futon is a cotton mattress used for sleeping. We unroll the futon on the straw mat, or **tatami**, that covers the floor. During the day, the futons are rolled up and put away.

My brothers with their baseball cards

Shoes are left in the front hall of a Japanese home.

Most of my toys and books are a lot like yours. Some of my dolls are special. In Japan, dolls are often handed down from parents to children. These dolls are displayed each year on March 3, or Girl's Day. Girls all over Japan celebrate this festival. I bet you're wondering if there's a Boy's Day too. There is. We celebrate it on May 5. Well, it's time to unroll our futons and go to bed.

Japanese dolls

CHAPTER 3

Around Shingu

Downtown

Shingu has very mild weather. Let's take a walk around town. We almost never have snow, but it does rain a lot. You might want to bring your umbrella.

There's a big downtown shopping area with lots of stores. Many of the shops are on a long street that has a roof over it to keep out the rain. Let's go to one of my favorite stores—the omocha shop. Omocha are toys. I love to look at all of the video games here.

There are vending machines everywhere! You can get all sorts of things in these machines, such as soft drinks, ice cream, and other snacks. Our money is called **yen**. There are coins from 1 to 500 yen. There is also paper money from 1,000 to 10,000 yen. A can of soda costs 120 yen. Snacks might cost from 100 to 200 yen.

Shingu is not a big city. But it is crowded. So a good way to get around is by bicycle.

A Helpful Visitor

See that beautiful Chinese-style gate near the train station? That is the entrance to Jofuku Park. Jofuku was a man who came here from China more than 2,000 years ago. His grave is in this park. The emperor of China sent Jofuku to find a medicine that would help people live a long time. He found the medicine but never went home to China. He stayed in Shingu and taught the people many skills. Some of these skills were how to fish and make paper. As you know, we still fish in Shingu. And people still use Jofuku's herb to help them stay healthy.

Gate of Jofuku Park

Our Floating Island

Have you ever heard of an island that moves?
Let's go to Ukijima no Mori. It's right in the middle of town. Uki means "floating." Jima means "island." Mori means "forest." The island is floating on a **marsh**. The wind makes it move. We can walk through the area on a bridge. There are many different kinds of trees and plants there.

Two Exciting Festivals

On the west side of Shingu, you can see a huge rock. Beside the rock is a shrine. Each year on February 6, we hold our exciting Fire Festival there. At the end of the festival, around 2,000 men run down the steep stone steps of the shrine. They carry flaming torches that they have lit at the shrine's sacred fire.

Ukijima no Mori

Another exciting local event is the Boat Race Festival on the Kumano River each October 16. Nine boats representing different parts of Shingu race against other. Each team trains very hard for more than a month before the race.

The Fire Festival

Our Beliefs

Shingu is in a region called Kumano. This region is sacred because the **kami**, the Shinto gods or spirits, live in our forests. **Shinto** is the oldest religion in Japan. It is based on the worship of nature spirits and ancestors.

A Shinto Shrine

One of the most famous Shinto shrines is in Shingu. It's called the Kumano Hayatama shrine. It is quiet and peaceful here, and no one is in a hurry. Before you enter you must be clean. No, you don't have to take a bath! You rinse your hands and mouth with water. Then you toss a coin into a box, ring a bell, and clap twice. Then you pray.

Nachi Falls

About an hour's drive from Shingu is Nachi Falls, the highest waterfall in Japan. Many kami are natural things like a beautiful mountain, a giant stone, or a waterfall. There is a Shinto shrine at the waterfall and a Buddhist temple too. **Buddhism** is another important religion in Japan. Inside the temple, you can see the great altar and hear the chanting of the Buddhist monks.

Shrine at Nachi Falls

Kumano Hayatama shrine

Our Leaders

Japan is an ancient country. Long ago, we were ruled by emperors. We still have an emperor today, but he no longer governs us. We elect many of our leaders like you do in the United States. All Japanese who are 20 or older can vote.

In Shingu, we vote for the mayor and the members of the city council. They take care of many jobs. They have worked to make our downtown better and improve our roads. They have built a new hospital. They prepare for emergencies, such as earthquakes or typhoons.

There is so much more to show you, but you will have to come back another day. I hope that you enjoyed visiting Shingu.

Good-bye for now, or "Sayonara" (sy-oh-nah-rah), as we say in Japan.

Here and There

Sister City

One thing that our local leaders do is make links between Shingu and other cities. Shingu has a "sister city." It is Santa Cruz, California. Like Shingu, Santa Cruz is a small city on the coast between the sea and the mountains. People from Shingu and Santa Cruz make visits to each other's communities. It is a wonderful way to learn about how other people live.

Glossary

Buddhism   a religion based on the teachings of Buddha

continent   one of the Earth's seven largest bodies of land—Africa, Antarctica, Asia, Australia, Europe, North America, and South America

futon   a cotton mattress used for sleeping

kami   nature spirits in Shinto

kanji   characters used to write the Japanese language

logging   cutting down trees for timber

marsh   an area of wetland

natural resource   something found in nature that is a source of wealth to a country

Ring of Fire   a great ring of earthquake zones and volcanoes that circles the Pacific Ocean

Shinto   an ancient Japanese religion based on the worship of nature spirits and ancestors

sushi   cold boiled rice rolled up in seaweed or topped with raw fish

A crinum, the flower of Shingu

tatami   a straw mat covering the floor in Japanese homes

typhoon   a powerful storm that forms over the western Pacific Ocean

volcano   a mountain formed by melted rock flowing through a crack in the earth's crust

yen   Japanese money

Index

Girls at a summer festival in Shingu